A GUIDE TOWARD THE SUCCESSFUL DEVELOPMENT OF AFRICAN-AMERICAN MALES,

2nd Edition

The Remix

Darryl S. Tukufu, Ph.D.

First printing December, 1997
Second printing September, 2008
Published by the Tukufu Group
Lakeland, Tennessee 38002

Designed by Tari Design
Printed in the United States of America

   Publisher's Cataloguing-in Publication
   (Provided by Quality Books, Inc.)
   Tukufu, Darryl S.
      A Guide Toward the Successful Development of
   African-American Males/Darryl S. Tukufu--2nd ed.,
   the remix.
      p. cm
      Includes bibliographical references.
      ISBN-13: 978-0-9662152-2-9
      ISBN-10: 0-9662152-2-2

   1.African American men—Psychology. 2. African
   American men—Conduct of life. 3. African American men
   --Social conditions. 4. African American youth--
   Psychology. 5. African American youth—Conduct of life.
   6. African American youth—Social conditions.
   I. Title

   E185.86.T85 2008   305.38'896073
                                QBI08-600205

Dedication

To my sons Ricky Joseph Tukufu and Khari Ture Tukufu; grandson Zion Joseph Tukufu, and the future men of their lineage. Additionally, to many of my male and female relatives and friends, who have contributed to my development:

Myra C. Tukufu
Estus Barham
Joyce Barham
Beulah Barham
Cheryl Golden
Stephen Golden
Petryl Starks
Edrice Clark
Yvette Kirksey
Wanda Clark
James Brian Black
Carmella Smith Weaver
William Bagley
Ronald Jackson
Daryl McDuffie
Ronald "Sababu" Miller
Gregory Andrews
Butch Harris
Charles Sitawisha
Sam Damu
Ernest Majadi
Reginald K. Brooks
Ronald Herndon
Robert "Oba" Penny
Herman Sawyer
Myron Robinson
Tamu Atwater
Goliver Malcomb
Robert Butler-Chochezi
Glenn Richardson
Walter Bufkin, Jr.
Barry McCoy
Rev. Dr. Otis Moss, Jr.
Pastor Horace Hockett
Kappa Alpha Psi Fraternity, Inc.

Bernice Starks
Peter W. Starks
Lilly Starks
Evelyn Thompson
Herman "Pete" Starks
Thirley Starks
Deborah Ingram
Henry Clark
Jeffrey Clark
Rose "Doll" Black
James Black
John Dean
Ted Bagley
Michael Jackson
Ernest Lokey
Lynnette "Kimako" Miller
Tony DeFoor
Kevin Williams
Karl Hekima
Amiri Jomo
John "Dadisi" Fuller
Cletus Moore
Sam Brooks
Sala Udin
Rhen Bass
John Jacob
Anthony C. Brown
Glenn Zellars
Frank Robinson
James Kimble
Darral Gaffney
Bishop Joey Johnson
Rev. Dr. Alvin O'Neal Jackson
Tavis Smiley
Dean-Freeman Clan

iii

Contents

v

Preface to the First Edition (1997)

For many years, I have been invited to schools, businesses, non-profit organizations, and religious institutions to lecture, facilitate and/or discuss a variety of issues. The topics ranged from race relations, diversity, and male-female relationships, to changing paradigms, visioning, and developing a positive mental attitude. I always enjoy the interactions with audiences on diverse topics, particularly when I believe that I not only contribute to the knowledge level of participants, but learn from them as well.

However, what has disturbed me the most is the tremendous difference of opinions expressed by individuals when the discussion shifts to the plight of the African-American male. This topic is compounded by guests on numerous talk shows who spend more time on the negative rather than the positive.

Therefore, reflecting on my years of involvement in such discussions, I decided it was time to write this guide. My background led me to writing this book for at least three reasons.

First, I am edging close to the half-century mark in age so have a lot of experiences from which to draw. At different times in my life I considered myself an integrationist, a Black Cultural

Nationalist, a Pan-Africanist, and a Democratic Socialist. I have

lived in poverty, been considered a member of the working class,

and eventually the middle and upper middle class. Additionally, I

was agnostic and/or atheistic until 1980, when I became a follower

of Christ. However, my religious affiliation has not restrained me

from being ecumenical when working with members of various

Christian denominations or other faiths.

My unique social background allowed me to live the

experiences of African-American males at various levels. Today, I

continue to hold a strong sense of dedication to my race, along

with a high regard for promoting the richness and diversity of all

people. To put it another way, I embrace diversity and

unapologetically endorse my Africanity.

Second, my academic background as a sociologist and

former professor of Pan African Studies or Sociology at the

University of Akron, Kent State University, Northeastern

University, and the University of Memphis, makes me more aware

of books and articles that portray African-Americans in a positive light.

Additionally, I have reviewed those publications that label Black folk as deficient in a number of areas, or state that all Black people have to do is pull themselves up by their bootstraps to make it in this world. Few recognize that some truth exists in all of these views, or offer solutions to the problem faced by African-American males. This background has helped enhance my analytical capability.

Third, I am the father of two African-American sons, one whose life I have nurtured as a step father/adoptive father, for the last eleven of his twenty years. My wife, Myra, and I also have a biological son who joined the family some eight years ago. Interacting with both affords me the opportunity to view how parental guidance supports development. Additionally, it is apparent that each, as individuals, has developed different qualities and abilities, and ultimately they will determine the extent of the development of these qualities and abilities. Parents and guardians must understand this, and not become the type of parents that steer their children in directions preferred by them. The exception, of course, is that parents should not stand by and allow their children to make choices that clearly would be detrimental to their development.

Parents must do all they can to raise successful and well-adjusted children, but each child must "do his/her own thing." Just as this guide can only offer parenting strategies for consideration, parents can only offer their children guidance to help them make good choices that will lead to good outcomes.

The main purpose of this book is to provide guidance and a model to parents, educators, religious institutions, social service agencies, neighborhood and community groups, fraternal organizations, penal institutions, and other organizations that interact with African-American males, on ways to inspire them to become a success as adults. Additionally, because it is solution oriented and emphasizes what can be done, this guide can be utilized by serious, mature Black males, high school age and older to aid in their growth and/or development.

Finally, I would like to especially thank my editor, Karen Hickman-Washington, who spent considerable time correcting my drafts. She went beyond the call of duty. Beverly Gaffney, who diligently worked toward bringing this book to life in print. Also I want to thank my reviewers. I respect and admire them greatly. They include: my pastor, the Rev. Dr. Otis Moss, Jr., listed as one of Ebony Magazine's Outstanding Black Preachers (Ebony, 1993); Paul Hill, Jr., a phenomenal community organizer and author of his nationally acclaimed book on "Rites of Passage"; Dr. Dorothy Anderson, renowned consultant for non-profit organizations and a mental health specialist; and Marco and Deborah Sommerville, an entrepreneur and elected official, and a social worker, respectively. The latter two helped keep the tone of this guide at an understandable level. And, many thanks must go to valued teachers and mentors such as Amiri Baraka, Clarence Barnes, Les Brown, Ernest Cooper, Dr. Edward Crosby, Dr. Ron Daniels, Ms. Marian Hall, Dr. Jeffrey Howard, Dr. Maulana Karenga, George Mills, James Mtume, Vernon Odum, Sr. and Vernon Sukumu.

Preface to 2nd Edition *The Remix* (2008)

Much has happened since this book first went to print 11 years ago. I am older, past that half-century mark, and my sons are older. The oldest has been blessed with daughters and a son.

Additionally, I received considerable feedback from numerous individuals young and old that read the first edition. Responses ranged from "thanks for steering me towards positive growth and development," to requests for additional information. A crisis of African-American males continues. Even Senator Barack Obama, the first African-American to become the Democrat Party's nominee as President of the United States, has amplified this crisis. He wrote one year ago in the National Urban Leagues' *The State of Black America 2007*: "The failure of our policies to recognize black men as husbands, fathers, sons and role models is being acknowledged, and we need a new ethic of compassion to break the cycle of educational failure, unemployment, absentee fatherhood, incarceration, and recidivism" (Obama, 2007:11).

This remix, or second edition, will read in part like the first edition, with editing provided by Meta McMillian, who edited my second published book *"R to the 3rd Power: Reflection, Renewal and Regeneration in the New Millennium."* This edition, however, will be greatly enhanced by 1) building upon the information provided in chapters from the First Edition, 2) further definition of the criteria used for guidance, which is now called the *Tukufu African-American Development Model*, and 3) including a chapter that will present various questions posed by readers of the first edition, and my responses.

The names of those who have encouraged and inspired me remain the same with some additions included in the dedicatory page. Time has not diminished the respect I have for all those listed, and their contributions to the cause of uplifting African-American males of all ages.

CHAPTER ONE *The Challenge...The Response: The African-American Development Model*

Twenty years ago, I conducted unpublished research on the behavior of African-American males. Initially, my interest was to study factors contributing to Black males becoming fathers in their teenage years. I consistently found patterns indicating that adolescents, and occasionally young adult men, were more likely to become fathers if they 1) lacked religious affiliation and/or did not attend religious services, 2) had the perception that "manhood" is synonymous with "being in control," 3) lived with parents and/or guardians who allowed them to raise themselves, 4) had an increasing sense of despair as time passed, 5) lacked educational achievement, and 6) had sisters who became teenage mothers.

Ten years ago, I read many articles (both in journals and in newspapers) on incidences of African-American male homicides. It became obvious to me that although many writers and journalists expressed many causes of homicide, that only a few looked at the

1

impact of culture. I determined that the cultural discussion had to be expanded because 1) many Blacks were killing each other because of a lack of cultural values in the African-American community, and deep disappointment of life experiences among Black males, and 2) that American culture, via the media, taught that violence and crime were tied to manhood. Furthermore, American culture and/or a lack of cultural values in the African-American community seems to imply that if power and success are denied through "legitimate" means, the response is to obtain them by any means necessary. Unfortunately, any means necessary includes the use of violence.

I then looked at articles on African-American male suicides which revealed that the incidence of suicides in this population has been considered to be serious for more than 40 years, and that rate has steadily increased over the past 25 years (Hendin, 1969). What I found to be just as revealing were reasons given to explain the increase. Some writers indicated high suicide rates exist and/or have increased because of family problems brought about by the absence of a father, difficult relationships between the mother and son(s), and unemployment (Davis, 1978; Hendin, 1969). Others cited a strain among middle to upper middle class African-American families as a by-product of integration (Davis, 1980; Kimmel, 1978). The thought here is that integration increased employment opportunities, and the buying power that results from this assimilation into mainstream society. Consequently, whatever problems White majority culture is experiencing will be experienced to a greater degree among those who assimilate into this culture, but who will never reach full equality with that culture. That realization exacerbates personal or family problems that already exist, and could result in tragic outcomes. On top of this is the stigma by some in the African-American community that suicide is not only unacceptable but contrary to the "African way of life." This attitude could be counter productive to a troubled individual seeking help to overcome thoughts of suicide, and learning to cope with the realities of life.

I can continue to cite negative life experiences of African-American males, like drug abuse, unemployment, etc. It's easy to point out the challenges to our success. What is more difficult, yet

3

more productive, is to engage in discussions or develop guidelines on what can be done to help these males achieve more personal success. Thus, I began to take notice of the extent that males were involved in specific activities or held particular beliefs or attitudes about life, 1) the more likely they were to develop with a positive outlook, and 2) the more likely they benefit themselves and their families, communities and society.

From my research and experience, I stated in the first edition that there are at least six criteria that strongly impact an African-American male's move toward successful development. I use the term "development," as defined by the Efficacy Institute in Lexington, Massachusetts, as the process of becoming a strong effective person by "building a sense of who you are and what you stand for; a belief in yourself and your abilities; knowledge of how the world works; skills to make things happen; and commitment to change the world for the better" (Howard, 1991). I believe if our males, young and old, are constantly engaged in personal development, they would have a profound effect on adverse conditions facing our communities. We might observe remarkable

4

changes in our families, schools and the broader society for the better.

I organized the criteria into a model that was called in the first edition, the *African-American Male Development Model.* Since that time, I have revisited the model and, because it also has been utilized for females, it is now titled, as indicated, the *Tukufu African-American Development Model.* Some changes were also made. The model suggests that development emanates from six criteria: 1) Religious, Spiritual, and Ideological Orientation; 2) Positive Mental Attitude; 3) the Nguzo Saba; 4) Knowledge of African/African-American Culture and History; 5) Social Development; and 6) Social Capacity.

An argument can be made that, with the exception of the Nguzo Saba and knowledge of African and African-American culture and history, the criteria could be a part of a development plan for all people. And, a case could be made for how helpful the other two criteria could benefit all people, by contributing to the knowledge of diverse cultures and history of everyone. This is true! However, this particular book will continue the focus, as did the first edition, on the need for the growth and development of African-American males. There are still too many being lost in American society. But, these tragic loses should not be construed to mean that only African-American males are maladaptive. History proves that members of any race/ethnic group, that have similar experiences, need support and direction towards positive growth and development. And, for the record, 1) Dr. Michael Eric Dyson and Rev. Jesse Jackson and others are correct when they cite the societal problems that put many Black males in the position we find ourselves, and 2) Dr. Bill Cosby, Senator Barack Obama and others are also correct when they discuss our own responsibility for being in situations in which we have not helped ourselves or should be helping ourselves.

As stated in the preface, the Tukufu model in the first edition has been further developed. It is now inclusive of African-American males and females. However, in this book the term "African-American" in the center of the circle in the diagram refers to the African-American male. Ideally, the qualities of each model criterion should be reflected in the Black male, and each criterion should be linked to one another. Thus, an African-American male can find himself displaying one or more of the criteria at any point of his development.

For maximum effect, with respect to growth and development our males should be experiencing all six criteria. Each of the six (Figure One) will be further explained in the chapters that follow.

Figure One

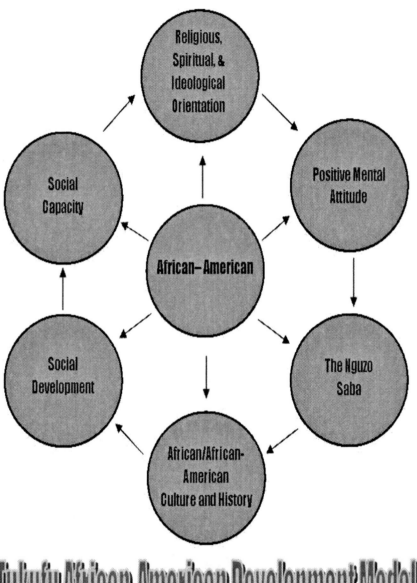

Religious, Spiritual, & Ideological Orientation

Social Capacity

Positive Mental Attitude

African–American

Social Development

The Nguzo Saba

African/African-American Culture and History

Tukufu African-American Development Model

CHAPTER TWO Religious, Spiritual, and Ideological Orientation

African people have developed a strong religious and/or spiritual base. That base started with African indigenous religions, and extended to and embraced the major religions of Judaism, Christianity and Islam. In America, the majority of Blacks identify themselves as Christians, and members of various denominations. An increasing number of African-Americans, however, are converting to Islam, from the Sunni to Nation of Islam sects of the religion. A smaller number of African-Americans adhere to Judaism. Additionally, other smaller segments of African-Americans have become followers of such Eastern religions as Buddhism and Ba'hai. Still others have become associated with forms of African spirituality, or African indigenous religions like Yoruba, which has a number of adherents from Pittsburgh to metropolitan areas farther along the East coast.

Additional views I have on this first criterion, "Religious,

Spiritual, and Ideological Orientation" can also be found in my book *N.E.R.D. (Nubian Elegance Rare and Divine): A Guide for High-Achieving African-American Students,* (Tukufu, 2002). Note, however, the subject matter of this criterion in that publication has changed slightly from "Spiritual, Religious, and Philosophical" to what I see as more relevant and important. Thus, the presentation in this book begins with "Religious," followed by "Spiritual" and concludes with "Ideological Orientation."

Religion has a spiritual base but, more specifically, is a form of service and worship of God within an institutionalized system with particular beliefs, attitudes and practices. No matter your faith or belief system, most religions have elements that direct you to a more positive life-style. This, in turn, leads toward high achievement. Additionally, religions are in an institutional setting and their teachings are largely included in sacred literature, e.g., the Holy Bible, the Torah, or the Koran. These publications are readily accessible as a reference for guidance and reinforcement of belief systems.

Various writers have emphasized that religious beliefs held

10

by African-Americans are grounded "within the social and historical experiences of the African-American community" (Lincoln, 1974). However, I recall readings in graduate school by Karl Marx, who said that religion actually is the opiate of the people, i.e., a drug that keeps them passive. I contend that although there are those who allow their religion to be an opiate, true believers of their faiths allow it to lead them towards positive growth and development.

I also would argue that we cannot use our religion to only help those who share our beliefs, or follow all principles of our faith. We have to be willing to assist African-American males in their growth and development regardless of where we find them on the religious or other scales. We must embrace them regardless of their educational background, social and economic status, bi-racial identity, and sexual orientation. To be "holier than thou" may cause, in fact could likely cause, us to lose them.

We all are spiritual beings, but how do we express, or acknowledge, our spirituality is the question. Those who say they are spiritual acknowledge that there is a positive, spiritual force that leads toward personal growth and development, morality, and high achievement. At the same time, there are many who say they are spiritual but leave it at that. They say they believe in a "supreme" or "higher" being but can't name "Him" (or as some have said "Her"). And many who espouse that they are spiritual lack a systematic way to worship or fellowship, to demonstrate their spirituality. They make some connection by visiting different religious services, whether Christian, Islamic or Judaic, but may lack a coherent process of following a specific faith. Figure 2 illustrates what I have called "The Alphabet Prayer" (Tukufu, 2000). Prayer is an essential way to reach religious and spiritual renewal. It is a means to talk with, give thanks to, and make formal requests to God. The Alphabet Prayer can assist you in asking for those qualities, attributes, etc. that are needed to become a God-inspired individual.

Finally, ideological orientation is more explicit than what I emphasized as philosophical orientation in the first edition. Philosophy deals with principles that are the basis for how we conduct our lives. Ideology refers to doctrine, opinions and a way

12

Figure 2   **The Alphabet Prayer**

I pray for continuous **A**…awakening to the truth of who God is and what He stands for.

I pray for **B**…balance that will assist me in focusing on all necessary aspects of life.

I pray for **C**…compassion that will enable me to understand others' distress and seek ways to alleviate it.

I pray for **D**…discernment that will reveal to me things that are hidden but divine.

I pray for patient **E**…endurance to stay the course and follow the principles of my belief.

I pray for **F**…faith…the ability to act on what I believe.

I pray for **G**…grace, the transforming power and divine assistance that will lead me toward spiritual renewal.

I pray for **H**…humility, the spirit of deference needed for the will of God to be visible in my life.

I pray for **I**…illumination that will bring about divine edification.

I pray that I will do all that is necessary to prepare for **J**… judgment day.

I pray for **K**…knowledge, which will lead toward good judgment.

I pray that I will be able to **L**…live the life of a true believer.

I pray that I will be forever **M**…mindful and provide assistance to the poor and oppressed.

I pray for continued **N**...nourishment that is provided by a strong spiritual base.

I pray that I will not be **O**...overbearing or quick-tempered.

I pray for **P**...patience in the midst of overwhelming affliction.

I pray for God-fearing **Q**...quality people to surround me at all times.

I pray for **R**...reconciliation...a changed relationship with God where my trespasses will not be counted against me.

I pray for continuing **S**...salvation and results, which will lead to a God-centered life.

I pray for **T**...truth, a constant pursuit of a transcendent spiritual reality.

I pray for **U**...understanding, composed of spiritual and intellectual knowledge and comprehension.

I pray for **V**...virtue, so that I can be a model of strength and an example of moral excellence.

I pray for **W**...wisdom, which added to knowledge and understanding, will lead me to God-directed action.

I pray for **X**...eXuberance, indicating that I am joyously unrestrained and exhibit enthusiastic faith.

Finally, I pray for continuous **Y**...youthful vigor to fight the good fight, to finish the race, in order to fulfill the necessary prerequisites to reach the ultimate **Z**...zenith marked by my departing this physical life.

of thinking. With respect to the purpose of this book, ideology relates to belief systems or formations that have African-centered or Afrocentric tendencies. This orientation includes exploring and taking pride in one's African heritage, and incorporating aspects of African and African-American culture into one's life to provide further enrichment.

Too often, I have found that some African-Americans, who try to "fit in" with mainstream society, fear embracing these cultural leanings. They tend to deny the importance of that cultural heritage, which is essential to self-esteem, self-worth and race esteem. They believe that they may be labeled "radical or militant," which may prevent them from obtaining what they perceive as benefits of being called an American. Others have also cited that they believe promoting Afrocentrism promotes a form of discrimination. However, I believe that Molefi Asante, who has probably written the most about Afrocentrism, says it best: "Afrocentrists have expressed no interest in one race or culture dominating another; they express an ardent belief in the possibility of diverse populations living on the same earth without giving up their fundamental traditions, except where those traditions invade other peoples' space" (Asante, 1993).

I use examples exemplifying Christianity in this criterion because it is my belief, and the one I am most knowledgeable about. Also, since my first writing, I have attended and graduated from Jacksonville Theological Seminary. I was ordained as a minister in March 2006. I have been able to share the Tukufu model via Men's Ministries, and Rites of Passage experiences. Moreover, because I have been associated with or have some knowledge of African-Americans of other faiths, such as Islam, Judaism, Yoruba, and Buddhism, I am confident the criteria for growth and development that I advance here can also be incorporated in those faiths.

Insofar as the religious and the spiritual sides of this criterion are concerned, there are at least four ways to enhance the successful development of our males. The first is by daily readings of the Holy Bible, or sacred literature associated with other faiths. These can be devotional readings, such as the Daily Bread or daily prayer calendar used by some Christians. If a young male is not

16

able to read, parents or guardians should read various religious

stories to him. Reading and understanding scriptural summaries,

and actual verses, are important. They can provide needed

direction to young men. Sacred literature has numerous examples

of how strong religious beliefs provide a basis for acceptable

conduct that is applicable to daily living and practice. For

example, citing references in the Bible that are very dear to me

(Ryrie, 1978):

Galatians	*5:22,23*	But the fruit of the Spirit is love, joy, peace, patience, kindness, goodness and self-control. Against such things there is no law.
	5:25,26	Since we live by the Spirit, let us keep in step with the Spirit. Let us not become conceited, provoking and envying each other.
Ephesians	*4:32*	And be kind to one another, tender-hearted, forgiving each other, just as God in Christ also has forgiven you.
	5:5	For this you know with certainty, that no immoral or impure person or covetous man, who is an idolater, has an inheritance in the kingdom of God

5:28		So husbands ought also to love their own wives as their own bodies. He who loves his own wife loves himself.
6:1		Children, obey your parents in the Lord, for this is right.
Philippians	*4:13*	I can do all things through him who strengthens me.

Second, Black males should attend as many religious services and classes as possible. I can recall the time after I finally professed my belief in Jesus Christ at age 31, and how for many years I had difficulty attending religious services. I was judgmental of people who attended church. I would justify my non-attendance by saying that I did not wish to fellowship with hypocrites. That is, "Sunday Only Christians." I came to realize that Christianity was based on one's personal relationship with God.

Other times I was convinced I could learn just as much watching television pastors, like the Revs. Frederick Price, Creflo Dollar, Bishop T.D. Jakes, and the late Bishop G.E. Patterson. Although I still enjoy watching TV evangelists, they do not replace engaging in fellowship. Viewing a program by yourself is not the same as being in the company of individuals who share your enthusiasm for life, God and your beliefs. Individuals build one another up, to become more spiritual.

By the same token, individuals seldom watch these programs in great numbers, making fellowshipping with others of your faith and/or belief even more important. I learned to appreciate the value of membership in a place of worship through my affiliation with four of the most dynamic faith-filled churches in America: The House of The Lord (Akron, Ohio), Mississippi Boulevard Christian Church (Memphis, Tennessee), Olivet Institutional Baptist Church (Cleveland, Ohio) and Born Again Church (Nashville, Tennessee).

Third, it is important for males to become active members in various established ministries, religious committees or faith-based organizations. These may range from Cub Scouts, Boy Scouts, and the Men's Ministry, to becoming a member of the church Usher Board. Some churches have social action committees and/ or community development corporations, which promote neighborhood and community activism to improve living conditions, support youth, strengthen families, etc.

Finally, a key component of religious orientation is talking to others about your faith. In Christianity, it could be referred to as evangelizing or testifying. This may range from organized neighborhood walks to one-on-one discussions about your religious beliefs.

As I emphasized earlier, I am a Christian. However, what aggravates me are people who include phrases like "praise God" or "bless you" in every sentence they utter. The same individuals you want to reach out to can be turned off by such frequent uses of these words. They can come across as sounding insincere or self-righteous. I learned years ago that it is often better to win the person over first than try to make your point. If you win the person you are in a better position to come back later to win your point.

I titled this chapter "Religious, Spiritual, and Ideological Orientation" in recognition that there are other belief structures that include development of African-American males. The ideological orientations I'm referring to here are Black

Nationalism, Pan-Africanism or various forms of Afrocentrism.

Black Nationalism invokes past and present history of Blacks, as a

means to encourage unity and progress together as a people.

Pan-Africanism, in its broadest definition, is a global

expression of Black Nationalism. Pan-Africanism advocates

mutual support and unity of people of African descent throughout

the world. Afrocentricity, mentioned earlier, has been perceived in

two ways. One is the use of Africans as the center of the universe,

so to speak, and the belief that all things of value, from inventions

to philosophy, were created by persons of African descent.

Another form of Afrocentricity concentrates on giving Africans

their "due," regarding their contributions to world society. But, it

does not negate contributions made by other races.

Many African-Americans shy away from any connection

with these "isms" or Afrocentricity, because of fear they will

develop, or increase, militant and/or radical tendencies within

them. Important here is that this orientation contains powerful

messages that are needed and must be passed on to our males, for self-development and race pride. It does not mean that African-American males will not be able to coalesce with other ethnic groups. Although I do not have membership in Black Nationalist or Pan-Africanist organizations, my past involvement causes me to be fully aware of aspects of these that cannot be minimized with respect to positive growth and development. All groups should have pride and dignity without becoming ethnocentric, i.e., believing that what they have is the only way and is best for everyone.

This chapter was designed to emphasize that strong religious, spiritual and ideological beliefs form the basis of African-American male development. They are the foundation for that development.

CHAPTER THREE   *Positive Mental Attitude*

If I were to rank in importance the criteria presented in this book, then positive mental attitude would immediately follow Religious, Spiritual and/or Ideological Orientation. For African-Americans – with a history in America fraught with periods of subjugation, oppression, discrimination and ever present racism – having a positive mental attitude encompasses both race and self-esteem. Moreover, I join others that argue that race-esteem may well provide the basis for self-esteem.

I have said in the past (Tukufu, 2000:34):

"...our self-image does not operate in a vacuum. So many other aspects of our lives depend on how we view ourselves. Our self-image affects our attitudes and behaviors. Essentially, the concept of self-image relates to how we see ourselves in our various roles. For example, I see myself as a Christian, a hetero-sexual, a husband, a father, a brother, an entrepreneur, just to name a few. In all of these roles I am perfor-ming at optimum when my self-esteem is healthy, i.e., positive. I have found that to the degree I am confident in my role, I am also competent. Thus, when the image of myself in a particular role is very good to excellent, I perform accordingly and vice versa. If my image is only good, fair or poor, I respond in kind."

However, I have encountered many individuals who discount the importance of maintaining a positive mental attitude, or either focusing on "self" or "race" to achieve success or personal growth. They believe it is "just feel good stuff," "nothing new," or "won't help eliminate racism."

I co-authored, with psychologist Deborah Plummer in a Gestalt Press text, a chapter in *The Heart of Development: Gestalt Approaches to Working With Children* that presented our findings on African-American adolescents and racial identity development. We stated at the beginning that (Plummer and Tukufu, 2001:54):

> "...for African-American adolescents, defining themselves as African-American or Black is an essential task to becoming an adult. Doing so requires a heightened awareness of what it means to be African-American in today's society. With that awareness, a conscious decision is made to 'become Black' and embrace African-American values."

Although the chapter was largely written to assist therapists with African-American adolescents, we pointed out the importance of racial identity "as a core and critical aspect of personal growth." This helps to explain the importance of this criterion.

As I emphasized above, race esteem has indeed provided the foundation for self-esteem. As a Black Nationalist of the 1960s and 1970s, I pursued group accomplishments and social change, but de-emphasized individual accomplishments. I developed a healthy sense of "group self-esteem" in the form of knowledge and pride of my heritage, however I suffered from a lack of "self-esteem," pride in myself as an individual. I could refer to many past and present accomplishments of African people, but did not know what I wanted to do for myself.

Not all of my associates experienced this problem. However, enough of us did. Consequently, when we pursued other activities, we found it difficult to cope or survive in new or different environs. Out of anger, or frustration, some became involved with drugs, returned to former illegal activities or returned to doing absolutely nothing. Many of us had failed to work on self-improvement while we worked on group improvement.

Today, I encourage some members of this new generation of Black college students, who are pursuing the same path. They can quote Malcolm X, W.E.B. DuBois, Cornell West and others and lead successful demonstrations. Yet, when you question them about their progress in obtaining their education they say, "It's not about me; it's about our people." On the other hand, I find considerably more students spending most of their time on career goals, but have little or no knowledge of their African heritage. These are the same students who find it difficult to cope in environments where they have to confront racism. Therefore, it is important to realize that growth and development must include self and "our people" for effectiveness.

Fortunately, those in the forefront of advocating for positive personal mental attitude are the motivational superstars of various race, ethnicity, and gender (Jeffreys, 1996). The number of African-Americans in this arena is increasing.

Some have achieved considerable success motivating people toward a larger vision of themselves. Les Brown is perhaps in the forefront of all motivational speakers, regardless of race or ethnicity, and in a field by himself. He was abandoned by his parents at birth and raised by a cafeteria worker, who adopted him and his brother. His upbringing was similar to many young African-American males, in the sense that as a student he was unfairly and unfortunately defined as educable mentally retarded. Les Brown's self-esteem was low, and he ended up receiving the D's and F's that were expected of him. One of Brown's high school teachers, fortunately, refused to give up on him. From that point on, Brown began to develop intellectually and his self-esteem greatly increased.

In short, there are at least four attributes that a positive mental attitude can provide. First, it helps prevent you from falling under faulty assumptions. An example here is the continuing poor self-image and identity crisis that exists among a number of dark-skinned people not only in America, but elsewhere. The assumption is that a lighter complexion is a ticket to upward mobility, both socially and professionally, and to having sex appeal. It happened when I was a child, and is continuing today, many young African-American children "dissin" (disrespecting) one another because they are "too dark." And yes, there are many examples where it works the other way…animosity toward those that are light skinned and/or biracial. As if individuals have a choice in parents and/or how they will look! On a micro level, a positive mental attitude prevents developing African-American males from having this poor self image or in judging others by their skin color. Secondly, you learn to develop the right approach to life and living. The right approach will encourage you to work on ways to be accountable and effective in your career, with your family and as a positive force in your community. Thirdly, you must develop the ability to handle change. This is important because nothing remains constant. You must be willing to adapt to circumstances you can't control, or those circumstances could wind up changing you. Along with this, we must develop the mindset to continue on our path despite adversity. Fourthly, create a game plan for success. This involves writing and, if necessary, rewriting goals. In the final analysis, if we are truly serious about personal development, we must seek it wherever we can and utilize all available resources. If we are motivated, moments of feeling

28

hopeless or defeated will not become the center of our being. We'll learn to change our strategy for development to fit new circumstances.

Dr. Jeffrey Howard, who heads the Efficacy Institute, created important principles to encourage personal growth and development that have proven successful in many school districts around the country. These guiding principles also provide a basis for development for everyone who is in a position to make positive impacts in neighborhoods and communities. His and the institute's concept not only make a contribution to developmental theory but also provide a process for application. They define efficacy as "the power to develop, to get better, stronger and smarter at anything that can help you build a quality life" (Efficacy, 1991). A quality life is determined by good health, positive relationships with significant others, wealth and freedom. Among other things, the institute has listed at least 12 "Efficacy Principles," its Efficacy Model, that when internalized lead to individuals maximizing their potential (see Appendix I). The basic premise of the Efficacy Model is that confidence and effective effort will lead to development. It emphasizes your ability to develop and get better in any area that you choose. Time and failure will not stop you if you are committed to your goal(s). Hard times will not set you back. Failure, or difficulty, is only viewed as feedback, because it informs you that you must exert more effort. The outcome is that you will be better prepared to meet whatever challenges you encounter.

Positive mental attitude and the principles of the institute are vital components for our journey to achieve personal growth. An entire presentation can focus on each point. I have repeatedly experienced the kind of impact positive mental attitude can have. Having such an attitude yourself pushes you to share concepts for growth with others. And that's worth the effort when those individuals approach you later and say: "I needed to hear that, I thought something was wrong with me" or, "I can identify with what you said, and I am going to really try to change my life." Responses like these make your efforts worthwhile, even though you may encounter some who are not receptive to your message.

For this remix, I believe I must add another source that I

was not familiar with during the first edition. Donald Clifton and Paula Nelson (1992) wrote *Soar With Your Strengths*, a book that escaped not only my attention, but also the attention of far too many others interested in increasing positive self esteem, growth and development in others. While working on this edition, I made presentations to members of education and business groups who were unaware of this text.

Clifton and Nelson's goal was to stress that we can all do better in becoming successful by focusing on our strengths and managing our weaknesses. Yes, managing our weaknesses. Sometimes we can get carried away talking about what we can do or become, but not contemplate the strengths we possess that make achieving these goals possible. As a consequence, we may then overlook, and not address personal weaknesses that can interfere with our ability to achieve our goals.

We recognize our strengths based on how much we seemed pulled or attracted to a specific activity, and how satisfied we are with the outcomes. We "get a kick out of doing it," that is learning the tasks we need to complete an activity in rapid time. We are able to glimpse our moments of excellence, while performing and excelling in that particular task or activity.

We recognize our weaknesses when we feel defensive about our less than adequate performance in an activity. We may not be able to make adjustments in a timely fashion to complete a task; we don't profit from repeat experience; we lose a lot of confidence in our ability to succeed; we cannot wait to complete the activity; and we can suffer some burnout by continuing to perform an activity, but not really reach the expected outcome.

Let me provide you with some examples. My strengths are in speaking, teaching, treaching (teaching and preaching), facilitating, and consulting. I feel confident in my abilities in these areas. I am satisfied with the outcomes I achieve. I get a kick out of doing it, and I am good at what I do.

On the other hand, my weaknesses are revealed when I try to assemble household items, when I have to use mathematical equations that are beyond basic accounting. My weaknesses also are evident when I try to play basketball. Yes, basketball! I do not meet the stereotype that "all" or "mostly all" Black males are good at this sport. Furthermore, repeated involvement in any of the

areas described above has not led to either becoming a strength.

However, as Clifton and Nelson have noted, you still must manage

your weaknesses. You can't ignore all of them, depending on your

circumstances. I have to develop budgets as part of my job. And

the budgets I develop are not simple ones. But, I manage, in a

sense, by surrounding myself with those who are strong in that

area. And what about basketball? Well, at least I'm a fan.

Let me propose some key action steps you can take to gain

and maintain a positive mental attitude.

1. Organize a personal and/or collective library, along
    with family members and friends, of motivational
    tapes and books.

2. Set goals for the number of books and tapes you
    will listen to a year. If you are not able to afford a
    good collection, local libraries maintain a collection
    for your use.

3. Put your dreams, goals and desires in writing.
    Highlight, or emphasize, those goals that excite
    you, that you are passionate about. Review them
    periodically, and make adjustments when necessary.

4. Develop and write a list of affirmations – positive
    statements – about yourself. Post the list in a room
    you frequent, or in various locations in your

apartment or home. Look at these daily, to help you develop a positive mental attitude and move to higher levels of development.

5.　　Find at least one person with whom to share your goals and desires. This should be a person with a positive outlook, or attitude, or is developing one. You will be able to inspire each other to pursue and achieve your goals.

CHAPTER FOUR   The Nguzo Saba (The Seven Principles

From 1967 to 1971, I was a member of Us Organization

and the Committee for Unified Newark (CFUN), respectively.

These Black cultural nationalist organizations had a profound

effect on my life. I joined the Los Angeles based Us Organization

in 1967, shortly after graduating from Los Angeles high school.

This organization still exists, and is still directed by its founder Dr.

Maulana Karenga. He continues to promote many of the same

concepts that were the foundation of that organization more than

40 years ago. The CFUN, under Amiri Baraka and based in

Newark, New Jersey, no longer exists. But, it was an affiliate of

Us, and adhered to the ideology created by Karenga, called

Kawaida, a theoretical doctrine that he indicates is based on

African customs and traditions reasonably applied to the African-

American context.

My involvement in these organizations was a part of my

search for meaning, certainly not the end of my quest. These organizations provided me with the grounding I needed to move from boyhood to manhood. My experience was the type of Rites of Passage experience for development that I will discuss later. These organizations, and their mission, helped me identify different ways to grow and develop particularly because of the emphasis on race esteem.

Karenga, who is still active and contributing to the study of African life and struggle for self-sufficiency, is probably best noted for the creation of Kwanzaa, the seven-day African-American celebration observed after Christmas, and the Nguzo Saba (Seven Principles), which is also referred to as a Black Value System (Karenga, 1998). The Nguzo Saba represents views and values that, when practiced, form one of the basis of continuous personal development (See Appendix II).

With the first Principle, Umoja (Unity), it must be understood that unity begins with self and then moves toward other points embodied within this principle, which involves people or groups coming together for a positive cause. This does not mean that you first get yourself together before moving into other areas, but it does mean that self at least has to be on the move toward development, as discussed in the last chapter.

Kujichagulia (Self-Determination) embodies the spirit of African-Americans determining their own destiny. It transcends the concepts of "going along to get along" and "don't rock the boat." Instead, we have to be bold enough to speak for ourselves as individuals and groups. It also stresses the responsibility to live up to the meaning of the names, particularly African and Arabic that we were given at birth. It is very disheartening to find that many of our young men arrested, for a number of different reasons, possess African or Arabic names that they fail to live up to the often noble meanings of those names. It must also be Kujichagulia, along with a number of things that would encourage an African-American male, like Senator Barack Obama, to seek the highest office in America. His win would be our win but we cannot expect that all will be right in America. Racism, sexism, classism, and other inequalities will not automatically disappear.

Ujima (Collective Work and Responsibility) and Ujamaa

(Cooperative Economics) compel us to work with each other with a collaborative spirit. These two Principles emphasize assisting each other in any number of endeavors, including each other's personal development, efforts to strengthen our families and neighborhoods, and conducting entrepreneurial activities together. Although it may not be spelled out, it also implies the support of Black-owned businesses.

Over the years, lack of support of our businesses has become a major concern to African Americans. In the past, many African-American businesses were community-based, and a majority of the employees were African-American. An increasing number of African-American owned businesses are appearing in the technical and/or service arenas that have a predominately non-African-American staff. Nonetheless, African-American owned businesses should still be supported.

The follow up to Workforce 2000 (Hudson Institute, 1987), Workforce 2020 (Hudson Institute, 1997), emphasizes the ever-growing meritocracy of American society. The report reveals that only individuals with the necessary skills and experience for increasingly technology and skilled service based markets will secure the higher paying jobs. We need to continue preparing our youth and other job seekers for this reality, by providing, or ensuring they get the training needed to move them into technical fields and other emerging fields, in large numbers. African-American males need to be ready to assume these jobs. If we, as a community, do not help prepare them, many may find themselves on some street corner.

Nia (Purpose) targets neighborhood and community building. I believe the reference in this Principle to restoring "our people to their traditional greatness" is key. It supports the concept that no matter what tragic or inhumane situations we have faced, we are part of a race of people that has always achieved greatness. I recall stories told about life in ancient Timbuktu, Mali. For instance, if a personal item was left at some place in the city, and if it was not dislodged by rain, wind, or other natural elements, it would still be in that place until retrieved by its owner. Although such situations were more likely years ago, there were some places within predominately African-American communities where you could leave your home unlocked. Is this a pipe dream for our world today, or can we once again get back this greatness?

Kuumba (Creativity) has become a matter of controversy within our diverse communities. On one hand we have artists that proclaim that the nature of their art, literature, or music should be personally determined, and they have the right to express themselves in the manner they see fit. Others state emphatically that what they create must be what Karenga refers to as functional, collective and committing. In other words, the creations should have a purpose, is done for the benefit of all and moves African-Americans toward positive change and development.

I applaud our diverse art platforms – Blues, Jazz, Slam Poetry and Urban Rap, as well as the increasing number of Black writers and film directors who distribute material emphasizing the everyday struggles of African-Americans. However, if we are serious about further development of African-American males, we should continue to encourage discussions about any misgivings about some artistic expressions, with the shared goal of presenting positive development messages that can be passed to future generations.

Let me state emphatically that I am not seeking story book endings to creative work, because many of our artists are right when they talk about "how things are in the hood." But if we are committed to serious development, we should communicate that development will be difficult to achieve if we call women the equivalent of a female dog or a garden utensil. I like rap as long as its messages are positive, when they affirm our ability to be positive contributors to our neighborhoods and support one another, and does not include profanity or encourages violence.

I composed two raps. One is for elementary school aged children and the other for older students. I prefer to have adults, usually parents or teachers, in the audience particularly when I present my second rap, "The Grandfather's Rap," since I include a message specifically for them. Figures 3 and 4 illustrate the two raps.

Finally, there is Imani (Faith). This Principle is the foundation, or impetus, for the Nguzo Saba. All of these Principles really begin with faith. Although Imani moves us in the right

41

TUKUFU'S RAP

Listen to the words I'm about to say,

Unlike Burger King, you cannot have it your way.

I came here today, to let you know,

Excel in school it's the only way to go.

Don't let no one say, "You don't have the aptitude,"

Just listen to Jesse, it's all about attitude.

So teachers I say, like Earth, Wind, and Fire,

Meet them at their need or it's time to retire.

So homeboy and homegirl stay in school and do your best,

Stay out the streets and all that mess.

Reefer, crack and alcohol ain't right in school,

And if it's your habit, you'll always be a fool.

So finally I say if you wanna be chillin,

Excel in school or you only be illin.

© 1989 Darryl Tukufu

Figure 4

THE GRANDFATHER RAP

I'm the grandfather rapper, couldn't be dapper,

Everywhere I go the people want to know.

They say, "You're too old to rap."

I say, "You take the nap."

Then they say, "Rap ain't the way,"

And this is what I say,

"You talk about the youth and the things they do and say,

You somehow got amnesia, cause you did it yesterday.

Communication is not a thing of the past,

You've got to talk the language for the message to last.

So listen to me carefully so you'll have a better day,

And I know I need to tell you they won't always have their way.

So don't sweat when they say, 'You don't understand!'

Tell them that you do but can't respond to all demands.

And although it's not easy and I'd be the first to tell,

Try to talk the language or they'll drive you straight to hell."

© 1991 Darryl Tukufu

43

direction, it is more than simply saying you "believe" in some-thing. Acting on what you believe in is true faith, because you expect certain outcomes as a result of your action (Price, 1976). For many people, if you "believe" then you have faith. For instance, saying "I believe our people, our parents, our teachers, our leaders and the righteousness and victory of our struggle" are progressively moving in the right direction to help our young Black males, and African-Americans in general. Are those beliefs backed up by actions? As we can see, this is not always the case.

The real question is how can we use the Nguzo Saba in the development of African-American males? There are at least three ways to proceed. First, the Principles should be displayed in prominent places in our homes, and at our work sites if possible. African-American businesses particularly barber shops, beauty salons, and some of the well traveled facilities within African-American communities, should be urged to place them in a prominent location in view of their customers. These efforts could serve as affirmations that some individuals need to get them in their subconscious, to recall at important junctures. They would be in a better position to move on Imani. For large printed copies of the Nguzo Saba, contact the African-American Cultural Center in Los Angeles, or local African-American bookstores. Better still, use your Kuumba (Creativity) and make your own.

Second, far too many of us discuss the Nguzo Saba only at Kwanzaa. For the rest of the year, these Principles seem to be dormant. One suggestion I would offer is to make the Principle Imani (Faith) a part of our daily religious, spiritual, and/or ideological belief system for daily activities. This is given as a starting point, since Imani (Faith) is the basis of the rest of the Principles. The remaining Principles could be emphasized in two-month segments during the year. For example, Umoja (Unity) would be emphasized in January and February. February being Black, or African-American, History month – as are the other 11 months - makes highlighting Umoja at this time all the more appropriate.

Next, Kujichagulia (Self-Determination) would be emphasized in March and April. This process would continue with the remainder of the Principles, with Kuumba (Creativity) being highlighted in November and December. Activities encompassing these Principles, during their designated periods, that do not exclude mention of the other Principles, could be planned for the home, Black-owned business or neighborhood.

A city, or region-wide, Kwanzaa committee could sponsor activities and operate throughout the year. This would require additional work for various individuals, but remember we are talking about development, which is a full-time job.

Third, the Nguzo Saba should be instituted and taught in all men's groups, from the Cub Scouts to Greek-letter Fraternities and Fraternal Orders, from Christian Sunday School and Men's Ministries, to Boys Clubs and YMCA functions within African-American communities. Additionally, many of the Principles can be used as affirmations to be recited by sports teams prior to competition.

CHAPTER FIVE *African/African-American Culture and History*

My first experience with the importance of culture was in the late 1960s and early 1970s, as a member of Us Organization and the Committee for Unified Newark (CFUN). Kawaida philosophy emphasized that culture determined our identity (who we are racially and ethnically), purpose (centered on our identity), and direction (emphasizing the manner in which we should be moving).

I attended Youngstown State University where I eventually earned my bachelor's degree in Sociology. During that time, I was able to witness more vividly the importance and impact of culture between and among people, despite their race or ethnicity.

Popular perception, perpetuated in some media and one's own perception, continues to leave the impression that there is one form of Black culture. That one form is some nebulous unanimity in expression of one's desires and outlooks on life that does not

47

exist with any group. What contributes to this misperception is the stereotypical belief that African-American culture lies largely in dress and entertainment. Culture is a way of life that cannot be divided into a few quantifiable segments of much broader dimensions that help define a people. African-American culture, as is the case with other cultures, is fluid. As was mentioned in Chapter Two, there are African-American Christians, Muslims, Buddhists, and those who adhere to various philosophies and ideologies. Such diversity in religious beliefs has developed over time.

History, therefore, is a necessary part of culture. The reason is simple. History details the life of a people over time, from their way of life in the past, to how members of that group live in the present, and allows us to predict what some cultural groups will do in the future. It also provides the opportunity for people to critique themselves, take note of their challenges, determine their opportunities and plot a course toward social development. Some change in cultural habits and expressions will take place, because the challenges and opportunities faced will prompt the need to make changes.

In order to promote African-American male development, our history must include more than information on when Africans supposedly arrived in North America, or on the shores of what is called the United States of America. Our history extends to another continent, Africa. The development of our males must include aspects of African history, as written in works by John G. Jackson (1970), Basil Davidson (1966), Yosef ben-Jochannan (1977) and Ivan Van Sertima (1976), to name a few. It must teach about the great Kings of Africa, and the rise and fall of the great states of Ghana, Mali, and Songhay. It must reveal information about the Great Zimbabwe, as well as Africa's link to Asia, Europe and America. Then it should highlight the accomplishments and contributions of African-Americans to the world, as told through books written by John Blassingame (1979), Hattie Carwell (1977), Harold Cruse (1967) and others.

During African-American History Month in February 2006, I preached a sermon at Olivet Fellowship Baptist Church in Memphis, Tennessee to begin the Sankofa series started by the

49

church. Sankofa is from the Akan language in Africa which means: "We must go back and reclaim our past so we can move forward; so we can understand why and how we came to be who we are today." My sermon topic was: "Are We Free?" As a part of this sermon, and with the focus on African heritage with respect to the Bible, I cited Genesis Chapter 10, which gives the descendants of Noah after the flood, namely the offspring of his sons, Japheth, Shem and Ham. The current human family descended from these three.

Africa generally is considered the cradle of civilization. That Genesis account reveals that Japheth's descendants – after time, selection, genetic variation, and their spread across Eurasia from the Black Sea, Caspian Sea and Spain – eventually became Europeans (or Caucasians). The account goes on to reveal that Jews and Arabs descended from Shem, and those that remained a part of the African descended from Ham.

But to emphasize the African, or Black influence, I remember attending a meeting where a pastor in attendance introduced us to a group called the Lemba. I followed up on his presentation with some research of my own and found that these people were/are Black Jews. They are different from the Falasha, or Black Jews, many of whom live in Israel today, and trace their ancestry to Menelik I. According to tradition, Menelik I was the son of King Solomon and the Queen of Sheba (Makeda), who was briefly introduced in the Bible at I Kings Chapter 10.

Research (google "Lemba") shows that the Lemba men possess a gene on their Y chromosome that may connect them to the Levi tribe of Israel, and that 2,500 years ago a group left Judea and settled in Yemen. These members of Lemba eventually moved to South Africa where a number of Lemba live today. Also of interest is that this group is believed to be descended from Moses' brother, Aaron. I believe that this, and other little-known historical points, exemplifies how knowledge can be important to African Americans. Such knowledge can enhance the self and race esteem of young Black males, and reinforce in all of us the important place those of African descent have in world history.

The following can serve as tools that can be used to show how culture and history can be utilized to assist in the successful development of African-American males.

1. Parents and/or guardians and various social institutions should invest in a library of books focusing on the African and African-American experience. Books referenced by authors highlighted above should be the starting point. Again, as mentioned earlier, if you cannot afford these, area libraries have or can obtain them from the publishers.

2. Organize reading clubs at appropriate reading levels of the readers. African-American women are more experienced with this, so should be consulted on ways to get such clubs started.

3. If classes, focusing on the African and African-American experience are offered at various schools, colleges, community centers, etc., males should enroll. If classes are not available, parents and the community should organize to make them a reality.

4. Encourage radio stations to follow Tom "The Fly Jock" Joyner's lead in his nationally syndicated morning radio program, which includes a segment on "The Little Known Black History Fact." However, the format you develop for your group should also include historical issues and events involving those of African descent from around the world. One station that I am aware of that includes a daily history fact in this manner is Hallelujah FM-95.7 in Memphis, TN, hosted by Michael Adrian Davis and Eileen Collier.

5. Encourage church or religious institutions to incorporate, as a part of the Sunday school curriculum, "African and African-American Culture and History."

6. Encourage sports programs, such as Midnight Basketball, which are usually housed at neighborhood or community centers, to provide mandatory African-American history sessions for their participants. Youth participating in these events should be obligated to attend presentations or discussions to take part in the programs.

CHAPTER SIX Social Development

I view social development, in the context of this guide, as forming relationships: 1) primarily between males bonding together through various experiences and programs, and 2) between males and females searching for positive and intimate heterosexual associations, and preparation for the possible results of these partnerships, i.e., children. In view of the importance of social development, I believe three elements are key: Rites of Passage, Mentoring, and Manhood Preparation: Relationships and Parenting.

Rites of Passage

Over the last 20+ years, the number of African-American males involved in Rites of Passage experiences has increased. Modeled after similar processes among indigenous groups throughout the world, Rites of Passage are designed to regenerate the community and prepare males and females to enter into manhood and womanhood.

Nathan and Julia Hare, founders of the Black Think Tank in San Francisco, published a guide for Black Male Rites of Passage that outlined a one-year developmental process for males from ages 11 to 12 (Hare, 1985). They described a "passage" as an initiation into manhood.

Paul Hill, Jr., director of the East End Neighborhood House in Cleveland, Ohio, also developed a process. But, he expanded his to include an Afrocentric Development Model, and create a national Rites of Passage Institute for males and females (Hill, 1992). This institute has expanded to include not only Rites of Passage processes for youth but Rites of Passage training for youth service providers. Both short- and long-term are available.

I was personally involved in a Rites of Passage process during my involvement with Us Organization. I became a member of the Simba Wachanga, which is Kiswahili for "Young Lions." This group was considered the youth and self-defense arm of the organization, and was offered to African-American men from age 15 through 21. The Rites of Passage processes of the Hares and

55

Hill emphasized community service, bonding, physical development, and learning African and African-American history. The main difference between the two is valuable in that it emphasizes the importance of this guide. Hill's process stresses that Rites of Passage is a life-long journey, not one-year or a maximum seven-year process that the Hares and Us Organization promote, respectively.

African-American males should participate at some point in their lives in a Rites of Passage activity. From the processes described above, the age for participation can range from 11 on up. Many opportunities exist. They can be found in churches, some Urban League affiliates and neighborhood centers in communities throughout the country. I was involved in a Rites of Passage process at Olivet Institutional Baptist Church in Cleveland, Ohio. Additionally, at the time of this publication, for three years I have assisted with the formation of processes at Mississippi Boulevard Christian Church in Memphis, Tennessee, and I'm working with a group of males planning a pilot program at two public schools in Memphis. From my review, many Rites of Passage processes include instruction in and an understanding of the importance of the following experiences:

1. Foundations of African Spirituality, Religion and World Views

2. Bonding and Team building

3. African and African-American Culture and History

4. Mental/Emotional Development

5. Physical Development

6. Discipline and Responsibility

7. Community Service

8. Initiation

The goals are to increase the sense of self worth and knowledge of what it means to be a real man, a greater knowledge and understanding of African and African-American culture and history, a stronger connection to the Creator, and a desire to build and develop self and community.

Mentoring

Mentoring is not new. The concept behind it is that one or more individuals act as a counselor, guide, tutor or coach to one or more other individuals, who are usually younger. The approach may be informal or formal. The informal approach can evolve naturally whereby parents, guardians and extended family members watch, guide and nurture their young. Let's not confuse mentor and role model. I mentioned in the first edition that I continued to come across young men who say I was their role model when they were growing up. Until they informed me, I had no way of knowing this. Needless to say, I am pleased to have played any role in the development of these young men. Probably the main difference between a mentor and role model is that the former allows for personal growth through a process involving interchange and support. The latter refers primarily to imitating someone you admire, which may occur without the knowledge of this experience by the role model.

Formal mentoring refers to the more established programs that can be found in churches and fraternal associations, and particularly in organizations such as Boys Clubs, the YMCA, and Big Brothers. These programs tend to formalize agreements between the participants, namely the mentees and volunteer mentors. These agreements usually call for the mentor to spend a minimum period of time with the mentee(s), and follow program guidelines. Formal mentoring programs generally involve participation in outings, informal talks or discussions, community service projects and tutoring. Opportunities often exist for the mentor to contribute more, according to his skill level.

Group sessions for mentors and mentees are another aspect of the mentoring process. The goal here is to improve group socialization skills of mentees. I have found these group sessions to be quite effective. Many chapters of my fraternity, Kappa Alpha Psi, have Guide Right Programs, which are mentoring programs for young males. We know we're on the right track. Over the years, we received many acknowledgments of appreciation from parents and/or teachers of the young men enrolled in our programs. Just as admirable is the establishment of similar programs by other fraternal associations, like Alpha Phi Alpha, Omega Psi Phi, Phi Beta Sigma, and Iota Phi Theta.

Unfortunately, there are aspects of some of these male

mentorship programs that I believe miss the mark. These programs should add elements that make Rites of Passage processes so important, such as African and African-American culture and history classes, and more emphasis on group bonding and team building. Many programs tend to focus more on the informal talks and outings to the exclusion of the other crucial components that I described above.

More mentoring programs are needed. We should both encourage more informal mentoring and find ways to expand our formal processes to other groups. Furthermore, we must train mentees to become mentors themselves. This will increase the number of males interacting with each other. Ideally, we want a domino effect to occur, where each-one-can-teach one.

Manhood Preparation: Relationships and Parenting

To some extent manhood preparation is present in many Rites of Passage processes, but seldom is found in formal or informal mentoring. When I say "manhood," I am not referring to developing what I call the "physical" man. The "physical" man is concerned with personal satisfaction; has very narrow views of

60

what a man or woman can or should not do; feels that females are only sex objects and prefers a number of short term attachments or connections with them; finds it far easier to make a baby than take care of the baby; and insists on proving that most men are physically stronger than women by striking them when challenged or embarrassed.

The "physical" man tries to live up to the tough man image. He is controlling, condescending and believes that exposing feelings is a sign of weakness or being a wimp. Based on those beliefs, he believes he knows how a woman should be treated, which is likely to be in a violent and controlling manner.

Of all the counsel points I make in this guide, the traits of a "physical" man may be the most difficult for many males to overcome. I've heard many of the excuses. A few examples are:

- "This is how I was raised. All the men around me acted this way."
- "Society is at fault. I'm nothing more than my environment."
- "If it's so bad, why do women go for it the way they do?"
- "What are you talking about? I am assuming my role as head of the house."

The sad thing about those statements is that there is some truth in them. However, being a long-time "physical" man does not mean that you can't change. Every one of the examples I offered about the "physical" man, with the exception of "making a baby," was me during my youth. I used all of the above excuses and more. Experience is not necessarily the best teacher but it can be the most painful. But, we must learn from our mistakes. We as African-American males, no matter our age, must reassess and reinterpret our relationship with women in more positive and beneficial terms! If we do not do this, our growth and development will be stunted.

So, what can we do to move away from the characteristics of the "physical" man? I believe that we must first define some attributes of what I called the "social" man in the first edition, but that I now call the "spiritual" man. The "spiritual" man, with God in his life, is the real man...the man we would want to be. This man is one: 1) who believes that he and his woman are mates concerned with satisfying each other physically, emotionally and materially, 2) who determines at the beginning of the relationship whether to entrust authority over certain matters, whether financial

or otherwise, to the one with the most knowledge or experience in

that area, 3) that understands that if there is to be a head of the

household, the truly "spiritual" man would assume his role, 4) who

understands that in a relationship and once a commitment is made,

it must be monogamous, and 5) who understands that motherhood

may be something many women naturally desire, but that women

should not be coerced to assume under any circumstances.

Furthermore, relationships established by the "spiritual"

man are exemplified by sensitivity, trust, care and mutual support.

In a sense, these qualities help define what it is to be a male. This

means breaking away from the influence of the "physical" man and

beginning the necessary process of turning us into the men we

should be for ourselves, families and communities. Additionally,

perhaps what best defines a "spiritual" man are characteristics that

I mentioned earlier, but, being a Christian, I would like to

emphasize again. Those characteristics are found at Galatians 5:22,

23. That is, God will produce in us the "...fruit of the

Spirit...love, joy, peace, patience, kindness, goodness, faithfulness, gentleness, and self-control…" if we allow Him (Ryrie 1808).

Thus, to help African-American males achieve social development, I propose the following actions:

1. From the minimum age of 11, all African-American males should participate in a Rites of Passage experience. The process can be similar to the one proposed by the Hares, but should, if at all possible, involve participation in the type of life long process defined by Paul Hill, Jr. (see reference section).

2. All African-American males should be involved in mentoring, either as mentor and/or mentee. All mentees should be prepared, at some time, to become a mentor themselves. Mentoring programs that already exist should be reinforced and enhanced with additional group socialization, and experiences similar to that of Rites of Passage experiences.

3. Relationship and parenting classes should be taught in schools, churches, and neighborhood and community centers. Additionally, seminars on the same topics should be held by fraternal organizations, school-to-work programs, penal institutions and all other groups that have a "captive" audience of African-American men. However, these must be presented with the goal of promoting the characteristics of the "spiritual man" in program participants.

4. Become more aware of our word and/or term choices. For example, stating "my baby's mama" or "my baby's daddy" tends to trivialize working relationships that should exist between the mother and father for the benefit of the child. Thus, as I have done, others should join forces with Atty. Anthony "Tony" Ferguson of Chicago, Illinois, who has

coined a replacement term…,"Parenting Partner" to help parents focus on being parents to their children although they have no emotional relationship with one another.

CHAPTER SEVEN *Social Capacity*

It would be unwise to promote these programs as a panacea for our young men, without also giving attention to how that growth can enable them to gain and/or maintain some influence or power in society. I call this gaining social capacity. This extra dimension involves preparing and empowering African Americans to make an impact at home and in society in general. To accomplish this, I will briefly address three areas that I believe are important in personal growth processes: Community Organization, Political and Social Change Organizations, and Economic Empowerment.

Community Organization

When I speak of community organization, I include references to neighborhood centers, neighborhood groups, and social service agencies operating within African-American communities or having a large Black client base. Many of these organizations interact daily with African-American males, and a number of programs focus on youth. They are typically youth groups, sports teams and sometimes advisory committees. These groups, directly, or indirectly, teach discipline, build confidence and/or develop leadership abilities among youth. African-American staff should advocate expansion of programs to include Rites of Passage experiences and/or mentoring programs. Additionally, these experiences and/or programs should operate like midnight basketball programs that are held throughout the country. These programs have mandatory programming, and usually presentations and discussions that youth must participate in as a condition to playing sports.

Many neighborhood groups, particularly block clubs and tenant associations, find it difficult to attract male members. This often is the result of too few men in the home to help encourage the young men to participate. However, if the mentoring programs operate as I propose, that is, develop mentors and training mentees to become mentors, these mentors could increase youth involvement in these groups and/or organizations. The mentors would teach leadership skills by example, and other qualities needed for development, and becoming a "spiritual" man as referenced above. Honorary memberships for mentors should be started so the mentors can provide additional assistance in recruiting Black males. Social service agencies should also become involved as they usually have more resources than neighborhood centers and groups.

Again, African-American staff should be in the forefront of advocating for developmental change in the areas they serve. They should contract with individuals or organizations with expertise in Rites of Passage, mentoring and other areas of development described in earlier chapters. They should collaborate, when applicable; with neighborhood centers, neighborhood groups, and other social service agencies to supply the needed resources to enhance the growth of African-American males.

Political and Social Change Organizations

I view political and social change organizations as vehicles that seek to influence policy or redefine power structures in society. These can range from political parties involved in electoral politics to organizations such as the NAACP, the Urban

League, Black United Front, National Action Network, Campaign for a New Tomorrow, Million Man March organizations, and others. Their ideology can run the gamut from the very conservative to radical. Many of these organizations are involved daily on issues of race, gender, and class that impact the African-American community.

Male involvement in these types of organizations has always been important, and usually they have held the top leadership positions. Admittedly, some leadership positions have been delegated to males because of their gender. One organization which only existed for a few years in the 1980's, the National Black Independent Political Party (NBIPP), reversed this trend by stipulating that their national, state and local leadership be composed of two co-chairs, one male and one female. The decision to operate in this manner was partly in recognition of African-American male chauvinism, and to refute the idea that men should naturally be the leaders. I thought this change in outlook was a good, progressive idea, and was proud to serve as the male co-chair for the State of Ohio.

The point I want to make is that leadership does not necessarily have to be the goal of our young men. But, they should aspire to being involved and participating in such organizations. Regardless of the political or social change organizations that males belong to, growth and development should occur during their tenure with the group.

Economic Empowerment

African-Americans have emphasized the need for economic empowerment and development throughout this century, but with minimum success achieving either (Trower-Subira, 1980). During the late 1990s, the National Urban League was involved with two conferences, one sponsored by the Cleveland, Ohio, affiliate. During the 1997 conference, the National Urban League emphasized economic empowerment as the "next frontier" for accomplishment in the African American community. This local and national focus by Urban League affiliates has extended into this millennium. Economics and/or entrepreneurship have continued to be addressed at subsequent national conferences.

The National Urban League has the resources and clout to keep our "eyes on the prize," through its 100 plus affiliates across the country. However, there are still some things that we can do not only to help with this agenda but do for ourselves. I suggest:

1. Updating, or initiating, local, regional and/or national "best practices" relating to economic development, empowerment, and African-American business utilization of these practices. These "best practices" can be used as blueprints for setting goals, and charting progress and results. Network marketing, a form of entrepreneurship where individuals build their businesses by networking with other entrepreneurs that are part of the same group, should not be overlooked as a valuable development tool. A great deal of work is needed for this activity, but it has proven lucrative to a number of African-Americans. In most cases, it is far easier to start a network marketing enterprise than the more "traditional" business.

2. Informing your males at an early age that the end result of an education does not have to be a job, that is working for someone. Let them know that it would be far better to utilize their education and skills to start their own business(es).

3. Looking at groups like the Washington, D.C. based TEDI (The Entrepreneurial Development Institute), or similar programs, to get youth started. TEDI's mission is "to empower disadvantaged youth, ages 7-21, by allowing them to develop their own small business, avoid drugs and crime, sharpen academic skills, and form positive attitudes about themselves and their communities."

4. Recruiting and involving more males in workshops and seminars on economic development and wealth acquisition. These sessions could be held in churches, and

neighborhood and community centers. Additionally, these could be added to the curriculums of mentoring programs and Rites of Passage experiences.

CHAPTER EIGHT Conclusion

There is no denying the fact that there are challenges to African-American male development. In Chapter One, I stated my interest in research, and involvement in issues regarding teenage pregnancy, homicide, suicide and other "social ills" affecting our community. My intent was not to simply restate the challenges we face, but to offer suggestions toward our successful development of African-American males. What I offer is a way to build a strong foundation and withstand pressures of underdevelopment, dysfunctional families, negative peer pressure and other obstacles. I have seen firsthand, and heard from others, that these suggestions can and will work. However, our African-American males must be committed to their development as well. What I have to offer is not the final discussion on this subject. Others must continue to make meaningful contributions to this issue with a plan of action, and not rhetoric.

I began with an introduction to what I call the Tukufu

African-American Development Model. Its six criteria, if internalized by males, would put them in a better position to make a positive contribution to self, family, community, society and yes, the world. We would be able to, as stated in the fifth Principle of the Nguzo Saba, Nia (Purpose), "restore our people to their traditional greatness." No one would dare consider us endangered! For maximum effect, our males should be experiencing all six criteria.

Let me paint a picture of my view of a developing male, one in his teenage years moving toward adulthood. I say developing because we never become fully developed. A developing man would be committed to and active in his faith and/or ideological viewpoint. He would have above average race- and self esteem, because he listens regularly to positive mental attitude tapes and/or books from his library, those that he borrows from friends, or obtains from the public library. His value system is a result of following the Nguzo Saba. He is aware of his African-American culture and the history of African people throughout the Diaspora. He is developing socially through past or present involvement in

Rites of Passage experiences and/or mentorship programs.

He respects and treats women as queens and equals, and avoids taking on the role of a "Playa Playa." He knows what it takes to be a responsible husband and/or father and if he finds that he has a child and is not married...he acts as a "parent provider." His social skills rank high on a 10-point scale because of his involvement in neighborhood or community organizations, and empowerment and social change organizations. He is politically active, even when because of his age, is not able to vote. But when he arrives at that age, he is a top pupil with respect to voter education. Lastly, he is constantly thinking economic empowerment strategies for himself and his people.

Specifically, the following will serve as point-by-point directives for the development of young African-American males, as emphasized in the previous chapters:

1. Read daily the Holy Bible, Daily Bread or sacred literature associated with other religions.

2. Attend as many religious services and classes as possible.

3. Become an active member of various established ministries or committees.

4. Discuss your faith/belief with others.

5. Organize a personal and/or collective library, with input from family members or friends, of motivational tapes and books. Set goals for the number of books and tapes you will listen to in a year. If you are not able to afford a collection, local libraries maintain a collection of these for your use.

6. Put your dreams, goals and desires in writing. Review these periodically and make adjustments when necessary, as your goals change or as you get older.

7. Develop affirmations, positive statements, and post them in a room you spend a lot of time in, or other places in your apartment or home. Review these daily, to help you move to higher levels of development.

8. Find at least one person with whom to share your goals and desires. This should be a positive person, or one who is also developing. You will be able to inspire one another to achieve your goals and dreams.

9. Display the Nguzo Saba in prominent places in your home, at work and African-American businesses. Emphasize the values of the Nguzo Saba year-round.

10. Make an effort to establish a city- or region-wide Kwanzaa Committee that would sponsor activities and operate throughout the year.

11. The Nguzo Saba should be adopted and taught in all men's groups, from the Cub Scouts to Greek-letter fraternities and Fraternal Orders, and from Christian Sunday School and Men's Ministries to Boys Clubs and YMCAs.

12. Parents and/or guardians and various social institutions

should invest in a library of books focusing on the African and African-American experience.

13. Organize reading clubs at appropriate reading levels. African-American women are more experienced with this, so should be consulted on how to start them.

14. African-American males should enroll in classes focusing on the African and African-American experience at schools, colleges, community centers, etc. If classes are not available, parents and the community should start them.

15. Encourage radio stations to include Black history points emphasizing positive images, and social and political issues and events throughout the year. Emphasis should be placed on Africans throughout the world.

16. Encourage churches and faith institutions to incorporate African and African-American culture and history as a part of the Sunday School curriculum, or other appropriate classes taught at these institutions.

17. Encourage sports programs at neighborhood and community centers to provide mandatory sessions in African and African-American culture and history, as a condition for participating in sports. Follow the pattern set for midnight basketball programs.

18. From the minimum age of 11, all African-American males should participate in a Rites of Passage experience.

19. All African-American males should be involved in a mentorship program either as a mentor and/or mentee.

20. Relationship and parenting classes should be taught in schools, churches, and neighborhood and community centers. Additionally, seminars on these topics should be

held by fraternal organizations, school-to-work programs, penal institutions, and other groups with a "captive" audience of African-American males. The classes must be taught by the "spiritual" man, as presented in this guide.

21. Community organizations, political parties and social change organizations, to the extent possible, should recruit and involve males for active participation and leadership in their processes.

22. Update, or initiate local, regional and/or national "best practices" for economic development, empowerment and African-American business utilization.

23. Encourage entrepreneurship at early ages. Use such program examples as TEDI, to get youth started.

24. Recruit and involve males in workshops and seminars on economic development and wealth acquisition.

Readers of this guide, when we talk about development we are really talking about life! It is either growth or development or it is death! Worse than physical death is the death of the mind. I will close this chapter of our lives with one of my favorite poems, written by Burton Bailey, which has become even more famous via Les Brown:

If you want something bad enough, to go out and fight for it,
To work day and night for it.
To give up your time, your peace and your sleep for it.
If all that you dream and scheme is about it,
And life seems useless and worthless without it.

And if you'd gladly sweat for it, and fret for it, and plan for it,
And lose all your terror of the opposition for it.
And if you'd simply go after this thing that you want
With all your capacity, strength and sagacity,
faith, hope, confidence, and stern pertinacity.

If neither cold, poverty, famish, or pain of body,
Can keep you away from this thing that you want.
If dogged and grim you besiege and beset it,
With the help of God, you will get it!

CHAPTER NINE Questions/Responses

In the preface to this second edition, I indicated that I would present questions and my responses from readers of the first edition. They are as follows:

You mention that parents cannot be blamed for what their sons do; if they have done all that they can to prepare them. Explain this a little more?

When children go wrong, I find that many people are quick to blame the parents. Granted, parents have the responsibility to contribute toward their children's positive growth and development, and serve as mentors and positive role models in the process. However, after the parents lay the proper foundation, their children must then be held responsible and accountable for their actions. Thus, if the parent, parents, guardians do all that they can do and the children, who by this time should be young adults, go in the wrong direction, we simply cannot or should not blame the parent(s).

You mention a number of groups, parents, etc., who have used this book to help youth. What were some of their experiences?

I have run into numerous people who indicate that they read the book and had their sons/grandsons/nephews read the book, then all would discuss what was read. If the young man was young, adults read the book and explained the contents to the youth. Additionally, the book, and particularly the African-American Development Model, has been used in group settings. The most notable experiences have been in the area of behavioral change, cultural and historical knowledge, and an increased respect for females. The behavioral change resulted from Rites of Passage and mentoring participation which I have been told by some parents or program coordinators that they have seen this change in their children or participants. Knowledge of African-American culture and history has also been explained to me as a benefit to those that had little knowledge and that this newfound "pride" has increased their race and self esteem. Although the responses I received were more numerous in young adult males who had read the book, I was pleased to hear that even younger males…high school through college age have indicated that they would treat females better and strive to become a "spiritual" man.

What has been the response of your putting so much importance on religion and/or spirituality?

Christians, and in some cases those of other faiths, have responded very positively. The only downside, if I can call it that, is that one of my distributors indicated that he had contacts that were prepared to distribute the book throughout the New York City school district. But, because religion was discussed, the use of the book was prevented in that environment.

You mentioned somewhere in your book that we must consider that growth and development of African-American males is important for all males, regardless of their background, including sexual orientation. Do you really believe gay men or even bisexual men can grow and develop?

I do! There are very few, if any, families that do not have one or more members who are gay, or even lesbian, bisexual, or transgendered. Growth and development must still occur! There is a scriptural verse that I think lends itself to explaining how important this is: "If I have prophetic powers, and understand all mysteries and knowledge, and if I have all faith, so as to remove mountains, but do not have love, I am nothing." (I Corinthians 13:2). I read a book by a former staff member of the Center for Christian Studies at Gordon College, who stated: "…those of us who are heterosexual need to avoid the easy path of just talking about homosexuals. We need to talk with homosexuals" (Heie 2007). Now, if the question behind the question is can this book "change" a homosexual to heterosexual? The answer is: "No."

81

This book cannot change an orientation. However, I have seen behavioral change even in heterosexual, previously very homophobic males, who have at the least moved from toleration of gays to some understanding.

Do you believe that your model is the best one to offer?

I believe my model adds to the discussion on African-American growth and development, but is not the only one that Blacks should adopt. I think a few of those that have and continue to make important points on this subject are Jawanza Kunjufu, Paul Hill, Lathardus Goggins, and Michael Wynn.

You mention the importance of race- esteem. Is this just something important to African-Americans?

Actually, race- and/or ethnic-esteem also should be important to others. Knowing one's heritage and having pride in it is not anti-diversity, prejudice or racism. The problem comes when folks believe their race or ethnicity is superior to others. Additionally, what enters into the discussion are those that are biracial. With respect to society…those that are "mixed" but have "black blood" are still considered Black. This book promotes pride in this Black identity but does not discount ones other identity. As countless of "mixed" African Americans…Senator Barack Obama, Sydney Poitier, and Halle Berry, one should not discount any of his or her being.

KAZI

Additional Work to Start You on Your Path

1. What are your religious beliefs, and spiritual and/or ideological orientation? (If you have none, skip to number 3).

2. How important are your religious beliefs, spiritual or ideological orientation to you? Why? (Skip to number 4).

3. After reading this book, are you willing to seek further information on putting God, faith, and/or other "orientations" in your life? If so, name three steps you will talk to accomplish this.

4. List seven books on positive mental attitude you will read over the next year.

5. Name one person with whom you will share your goals and desires, to help keep you focused.

6. Name three friends you will share your knowledge of the Nguzo Saba (Seven Principles) with, and help them understand these Principles.

7. List seven books on the African and African-American experience, that specifically emphasize culture and history that you will read over the next year.

8. Have you ever been involved in a Rites of Passage process? If you have, name three of your most lasting memories of this experience.

83

If you have not, conduct research on Rites of Passage processes in your area that could benefit you or a male in your life. (For further information on processes in your area, contact the National Rites of Passage Institute, c/o East End Neighborhood House, 2749 Woodhill Rd., Cleveland, Ohio 44104)

9. List your mentor(s) or mentee(s). If you do not have one, seek one out as soon as possible. With your mentor, write down five things you will do over the next year, based on suggestions from this guide.

10. Prior to reading this guide, you probably had beliefs about how a male is supposed to act. If it applies to you and you are at the age/stage of a relationship, name the ways you will begin to interact with females based on the definition of the "spiritual" man.

11. Name one community or neighborhood organization that you will volunteer with, for one of their projects or programs during the next year.

12. Name three business ventures that interest you. Research the businesses in your area. Contact the owners and interview them about what it takes to be successful in those enterprise(s). Identify the steps you need to take to prepare you to own one of these businesses, or own another one, if you change your mind at some point about your first choice.

Appendix I

1. Development is the foundation of a quality life.

2. Smart is not something you are. Smart is something you get.

3. Developed people are educated and principled.

4. Do not bring low. Build up.

5. If you think you can, and you work hard, you can get smart.

6. Thoughts lead to action.

7. Use feedback to find your learning zone.

8. When you have a failure, or experience difficulty, learn to separate the information from the emotions.

9. Use positive "other influences" to support your development. Do not let negative "other influences" stop you.

10. Use the process of development to get to the zone of development.

11. Find out how good you can be.

12. Control your weak side. Choose your strong side.

13. Commit to your development. Choose to live a quality life.

Efficacy: The High School Curriculum
The Efficacy Institute, Lexington, MA
Copyright 1991, pgs. 269,270

Appendix II

Nguzo Saba
(The Seven Principles)

1. **Umoja (Unity)**
   To strive for and maintain unity in the family, community, nation and race.

2. **Kujichagulia (Self-determination)**
   To define ourselves, name ourselves, create for ourselves and speak for ourselves, instead of being defined, named, created for and spoken for by others.

3. **Ujima (Collective Work and Responsibility)**
   To build and maintain our community together, and make our sisters and brothers problems our problems and to solve them together.

4. **Ujamaa (Cooperative Economics)**
   To build and maintain our own stores, shops and other businesses and to profit from them together.

5. **Nia (Purpose)**
   To make our collective vocation the building and developing of our community, in order to restore our people to their traditional greatness.

6. **Kuumba (Creativity)**
   To do always as much as we can, in the way we can, in order to leave our community more beautiful and beneficial than we inherited it.

7. **Imani (Faith)**
   To believe with all our heart in our people, our parents, our teachers, our leaders and the righteousness and victory of our struggle.

Maulana Karenga
Kwanzaa: A Celebration of Family, Community and Culture,
Commemorative Edition   Los Angeles: University of Sankore 1998

References

Asante, Molefi. 1993.
www.worldagesarchives.com/Reference_Links/Afrocentricity.htm

Ben-Jochannan, Yosef A.A. 1977. Africa: Mother of Western
   Civilization. New York: Alkebu-lan Associates.

Blassingame, John. 1979. The Slave Community. New York:
   Oxford University Press.

Carwell, Hattie. 1977. Blacks in Science. Hicksville, New York:
   Exposition Press.

Clifton, Donald O. and Paula Nelson. 1992. Soar With Your
   Strengths. New York: Dell Publishing.

Cruse, Harold. 1967. Crisis of the Negro Intellectual. New York:
   William Morrow & Co.

Davis, Robert. 1978. "Black Suicide in the Seventies: Current
   Trends and Perspectives," *Institute for Research on Poverty
   Discussion Paper* No. 483-78.

Davis, Robert. 1980. "Suicide Among Young Blacks: Trends and
   Perspectives." *Phylon* Vol. 41, No. 3 (3rd quarter), pp. 223-
   229.

Davidson, Basil. 1966. A History of West Africa in the
   Nineteenth Century. Garden City, New York:
   Doubleday & Co.

Ebony. November 1973.

Fraser, George F. 1996. Success Runs in Our Race: The Complete Guide to Networking in the African American Community. New York: Avon Books.

Hare, Nathan & Julia. 1985. Bringing the Black Boy to Manhood. San Francisco, CA: Black Think Tank.

Heie, Harold. 2007. Learning to Listen, Ready to Talk. Lincoln, NE: iUniverse.

Hendin, Herbert. 1969. Black Suicide. New York: Basic Books.

Hill, Paul, Jr. 1992. Coming of Age: African-American Male Rites of Passage. Chicago, Illinois: African American Images.

Hudson Institute. 1987. Work Force 2000. Indianapolis, IN: Hudson Institute.

Hudson Institute. 1997. Work Force 2020. Indianapolis, IN: Hudson Institute.

Jackson, John G. 1970. Introduction to African Civilization. New York: Carol Publishing Group.

Jeffreys, Michael. 1996. Success Secrets of the Motivational Superstars. Rocklin, CA: Prima Publishing.

Karenga, Maulana. 1998. Kwanzaa: A Celebration of Family, Community and Culture, Commemorative Edition. Los Angeles: University of Sankore.

ʿimmel, Roberta. 1978. Black Suicide: An Epidemic? Focus Vol. 3:1.

C. Eric. 1974. The Black Experience in Religion. ʿden City, New York: Anchor Books.

Obama, Barack. 2007. "Forward." In The State of Black America 2007. New York: National Urban League.

Plummer, Deborah L. and Darryl S. Tukufu. 2001. "Enlarging the Field: African-American Adolescents in a Gestalt Context," In The Heart of Development...Gestalt Approaches to Working with Children, Adolescents and Their Worlds, Volume II" Adolescence." edited by Mark McConville and Gordon Wheeler. Hillsdale, NJ: The Analytic Press.

Price, Frederick K.C. 1976. How Faith Works. Tulsa, Oklahoma: Harrison House.

Ryrie, Charles Caldwell. 1978. The Ryrie Study Bible. Chicago, IL: The Moody Institute.

Trower-Subira, George. 1980. Black Folks' Guide to Making Big Money in America. Newark, New Jersey: Very Serious Business Enterprises.

Tukufu, Darryl S. 1997. A Guide Toward the Successful Development of African-American Males. Richmond Heights, Ohio: The Tukufu Group.

Tukufu, Darryl S. 2000. R to the 3rd Power: Reflection, Regeneration and Revitalization in the New Millennium. Richmond Heights, Ohio: The Tukufu Group.

Tukufu, Darryl S. 20002. N.E.R.D. Nubian Elegance Rare and Divine: A Guide for High-Achieving African-American Students. Unionville, NY: Royal Fireworks Press.

Van Sertima, Ivan. 1976. They Came Before Columbus. New York: Random House.

ABOUT THE AUTHOR

Darryl S. Tukufu, a husband, father, sociologist, ordained minister, entrepreneur, and community leader has served effectively in numerous positions with organizations throughout the United States. He was involved in the Black cultural nationalist and Urban League movements, and has received numerous awards for his advocacy and service to youth and the economically disadvantaged. He has served as President and CEO of non-profit groups, a professor and administrator at universities, a manager of departments in government, and is a life member of the NAACP and Kappa Alpha Psi Fraternity, Inc. Additionally, he has served on numerous boards and committees including the National Civil Rights Museum, and the Nike External Minority Affairs Review Board.

Dr. Tukufu received his A.B. degree from Youngstown State University, an M.A. and Ph.D. from the University of Akron, and a Doctorate of Ministry degree from Jacksonville Theological Seminary. He is credited with the following motivational raps for youth: "Tukufu's Rap" and the "Grandfather Rap." He is the thor of "Jesse Jackson and the Rainbow Coalition: Working s Movement or Reform Politics" published May, 2002, in nity and Society; co-authored "Enlarging the Field: African-n Adolescents in a Gestalt Context," with Deborah L. nd published in The Heart of Development Gestalt

Approaches to Working with Children, Adolescents and Their
Worlds Volume II: Adolescence edited by Mark McConville and
Gordon Wheeler. Additionally, he is the author of R to the 3rd
Power: Reflection, Regeneration and Revitalization in the New
Millennium, and NERD (Nubian Elegance Rare and Divine): A
Guide for High Achieving African-American Students.

ISBN: 978-0-9662152-2-9